Learning Islam

SANIYASNAIN KHAN
MARYAM KINTE

EDITED BY
SHAMSHAD M KHAN

Goodword**k**idz
Helping you build a family of faith

In the Beginning

Long long ago, there was no earth, no sky, no sun or moon. There was just darkness.

When Allah said, "Be!" all the galaxies and stars began to spread out into the darkness.

Then our bright sun and the earth and the moon came to be. Allah wanted this to happen, so it happened.

The dry land began to emerge above the seas and oceans. The lovely blue sky spread up above them and plants and animals began to appear. What a lovely world!

Muslims thank Allah for making such a beautiful world and should help to keep planet Earth and everything around us clean and green.

The First Man and Woman

When Allah created the first human being, He collected the best essence of clay and mixed it like potter's clay. Shaping it into a human being, Allah breathed some of his spirit into it. In this way He gave life to the first man and to the first woman as well.

Allah named the man Adam. He was the first Prophet. His wife was Eve (or *Hawwa* in Arabic). She was his helper and loving companion.

All people on earth belong to the same great family. All human beings are children of Adam and Allah created Adam. We should, then, respect each and every person and never look down on others, or speak rudely to them.

After all, we all have the same forefather – the Prophet Adam, and Eve is our mother. May peace be upon both of them.

Allah's Best Friend

Over thousands of years, Allah has sent many prophets to remind peop
about Himself and how to live a good life. About 4,000 years ago a
child was born in Ur, a place in what is now Iraq. His name was
Abraham (or Ibrahim). He was one of Allah's prophets. He believed in
Allah and was gracious and kind-hearted. Allah gave him wisdom whe
he was still a small child. He was so close to Allah that he is called
"Allah's best friend". Abraham used to tell the people a story. He said
that one night, while looking at the sky, he saw a particularly bright sta
so he said: "This is my Lord". But when the star set, he said: " I do not
love that which fades." After seeing the moon and even the brilliant su
setting, Abraham said, "I will turn my face to Him who has created the
heavens and the earth, and lead a righteous life." In this way Abraham
(upon whom be peace) taught people not to worship things created by
Allah, but to worship Allah Alone.

We Believe in Angels

Angels are made of a special kind of light. Allah created them to carry out many different tasks for Him. Angels know what they are doing and are obedient to Allah. There is no such thing as a bad angel. The angels are friends of the believers. The foremost is Angel Gabriel (or Jibril) who passed on Allah's words to the Prophets. Other angels help the natural world, like Michael (Mikail) who brings down the rain. The Angel Azrael (Izrail) carries off our souls when we die. He is the Angel of Death. Another is called Israfil. His duty is to blow the trumpet on the Last Day. At its sound the earth will fall apart.

Each person has an angel who writes down in a book his or her good deeds and another angel who writes down his or her bad deeds. Prophet Muhammad said that if somebody tells a lie, due to its bad smell, the angels run several miles away from him! So a Muslim should not annoy them by doing bad deeds. Muslims believe that God Almighty will see everyone's 'good and bad deed books' on Judgement Day, so each day a Muslim prays to Him for forgiveness and tries, with His help, to do better next time.

Belief in the Prophets

A necessary part of Islam is to believe in all the prophets. Allah has sent many prophets to remind people how to follow the right path. They all brought essentially the same message. The Qur'an names 25 of them. Some of these are, in English and Arabic:

Adam	- Adam	Jacob	- Yaqub	Solomon	- Suleiman
Noah	- Nuh	Joseph	- Yusuf	Jonah	- Yunus
Abraham	- Ibrahim	Job	- Ayyub	Zachariah	- Zakariya
Lot	- Lut	Moses	- Musa	John	- Yahya
Ishmael	- Isma'il	Aaron	- Harun	Jesus	- Isa
Isaac	- Ishaq	David	- Dawud	Muhammad	- Muhammad

Through Angel Gabriel, Allah gave some prophets a special revelation or "Holy Book", which was a confirmation, reminder and update of what came earlier. Other prophets taught what had already been sent in earlier Holy Books.

Some Holy Books named in the Qur'an are:

The *Suhuf* or Scrolls of Abraham. Some of the inspired prayers of Abraham are quoted in the Qur'an.

The *Taurat* or Torah of Moses. Much of this can be found in the first five books of the Bible, along with other material.

The *Zaboor* or Psalms of David. Some of these can be found in The Book of Psalms in the Bible, together with other psalms.

The *Injeel, Gospel* or "Good News" of Jesus. Some of this can be found in the Gospels according to Matthew, Mark, Luke and John, along with other material.

The *Qur'an* of Muhammad. The Qur'an is the Holy Book received by Muhammad, with nothing added, taken away or changed.

How the Quran Came to Us

One night, the Prophet Muhammad was sitting alone in the cave of Hira, near Makkah, to pray and think deeply. Suddenly, the Archangel Gabriel (Jibril) appeared before him in human form and taught him the very first words of the Quran. In this way the Quran began to be revealed by Allah to the Prophet Muhammad through the angel. It took 23 long years to complete all the chapters of the holy Book. Whenever new verses of the Quran were revealed, the companions of the Prophet Muhammad would memorize them and write them down. Finally, when all the chapters were complete, the Quran was made into the book form which we have today. Being the true word of Allah in human language, the Quran is a book of learning for all humankind which will last forever.

The Quran provides correct and simple answers to all the central questions which arise in a mind which seeks answers. It serves as a guiding light, inspiring and leading the devout people along the right path. The guidance given in the Quran is one of a kind and a great blessing to humankind from Allah, because it shows people the path to final success. It tells people how to behave, so that in the life after death they may enter Paradise, which is the final goal of all believers.

The Handwriting of the Quran

The Quran was originally written by hand on the leaves of date palms and parchment.

Most of the early copies of the Quran were written in a script with square-shaped letters known as Kufic, after the city of Kufa in Iraq. Later, many developments took place in the style of the Quran's handwriting but not one word has been added, taken away or replaced. Sometimes the letters are decorated with the most intricate designs in gold, silver and brilliant colours.

The Pillars of Faith

There are five basic duties or pillars of Islam. They are meant to help human beings feel a lifelong piety and devotion to Allah. These five pillars are as follows:

1. Faith (or *Iman*)

2. Five Daily Prayers (or *Salat*)

3. Fasting during Ramadan (or *Sawm*)

4. Charity (or *Zakat*)

5. The Pilgrimage to Makkah (or *Hajj*) at least once in a lifetime.

We shall be reading about some of these pillars in more detail in the following pages.

The Prayer to Allah, the Merciful

There are five daily prayers which every Muslim, male and female, must say at their appointed times. These are the names of the five prayers:

1. Early morning (or *Fajr*) prayer. It is said before sunrise.
2. Noon (or *Zuhr*) prayer. It is said between noon and mid-afternoon.
3. Afternoon (or *Asr*) prayer. It is said between mid-afternoon and sunset.
4. Sunset (or *Maghrib*) prayer. It is said just after sunset.
5. Evening (or *Isha*) prayer. It is said at night.

Before praying we should wash our hands, face and feet. This is called ablution or *wudu*. Each prayer takes 5-10 minutes to complete. Verses from the Quran are repeated in the prayer which glorify and praise Allah. Prayers bring us nearer to Allah and help us avoid doing wrong.

In each prayer Muslims ask Allah to exalt and bless Muhammad as He exalted and blessed Abraham, peace be upon them both. The Quran tells us that Islam is the religion of Abraham.

Let's Make A Visit to the Mosque

Mosques are buildings that are specially used for the prayers which are held five times a day. Apart from that, mosques fulfil other functions in the Muslim community: religious discussions take place and religious schools are sometimes run at weekends.

Some mosques house a library and a museum as well. In some bigger mosques there is a separate prayer hall for the women.

A mosque has a washing area where worshippers wash their hands, face and feet before going for prayer. Most of the older mosques have a courtyard. There is a prayer hall. The mosques generally have a dome and one or more minarets. The walls, ceilings and roof of some mosques are adorned with verses from the Quran in beautiful handwriting.

Some of the world's most beautiful mosques are found in Makkah, Madinah, Jerusalem, Istanbul, Delhi, Cairo, Damascus, Dubai, Lahore, Kuala Lumpur, London, Birmingham, New York, Paris, Toronto and many other places.

Belief in One God

'Allah' means 'The God'. The Quran tells us that God is One. It reminds us that Allah is the source of all justice, forgiveness and kindness. Everybody and everything needs Him while He needs no one. He was never born and He will never die. He just is.

In the Quran a very short chapter, Surah Ikhlas, says:

> *Say: 'He is Allah. He is One.*
> *He needs nothing,*
> *but all others need Him.*
> *He was not born and*
> *He is not parent to any children.*
> *Nobody and no thing is like Him.'*

Allah is so Great. Nothing can be like the Maker and Sustainer of the whole universe.

The Throne of the Merciful

There is a verse in the Quran which is known as The Verse of the Throne (or *Ayat al-Kursi*). In this verse Allah describes Himself in the most powerful and thrilling words. This beautiful verse tells us of the glory and majesty of the Creator and prompts us to submit to His will.

Here is an English translation of parts of the Verse of the Throne:

Allah! There is no god other than He,

The Living, the Everlasting, the Eternal.

No slumber can seize Him nor sleep.

His Throne extends over the heavens and the earth.

To Him belongs whatever is in the

heavens and on the earth.

He is the Most High,

The Supreme One

The Holy Kabah

The Kabah was built by the Prophet Abraham (Ibrahim) about 4000 years ago. The Kabah stands in the centre of the Grand Mosque at Makkah. It is towards the Kabah that, five times every day, more than a quarter of the world's population turn themselves in prayer.

The Kabah is about 50 feet high and about 40 feet in width. It is built of grey-stone taken from the surrounding hills of Makkah. At one of the corners an oval-shaped black stone is fixed in the wall. It is known as the Black Stone, and was originally set there by the Prophet Abraham. The four walls of the Kabah are covered with a black brocaded covering called the *kiswa*. The *kiswa* is decorated with verses from the Quran written in beautiful golden handwriting. Inside the Kabah there are three wooden pillars which support the roof. The walls and the floor are covered with marble. Neither the Kabah nor the Black Stone is an object of worship.

What Is A Muslim Prayer Like?

The prayer Muslims pray most often is called "Al Fatihah".
It means "The Opening" and it is the first chapter in the Quran. Muslims pray it at least 17 times a day.

Al Fatihah

In The Name of Allah, The Most Kind, The Most Merciful:

All praise is for Allah,
Lord of the worlds,
The Most Kind, The Most Merciful,
Ruler of the Day of Judgement.

You alone we worship and You alone we ask for help.
Keep us on the straight path,
the path of those whom You have blessed, not of those who invite Your
wrath, nor of those who go astray.

The Prophet's Mosque

The Prophet's Mosque at Madinah is one of the three most holy mosques. The other two are at Makkah and Jerusalem. This mosque was originally built by the Prophet Muhammad and his companions in the 6th century C.E. Originally the mosque was made from the trunks of palm trees. Since then the mosque has been extended several times. Today this is the world's largest mosque with an area of more than 400,000 square metres where more than one million worshippers can pray at one time.

The Prophet Muhammad used to preach the message of the Quran in this mosque. Beside the prayer hall are the graves of the Prophet Muhammad and Caliphs Abu Bakr and Umar. A visit to this mosque gives great happiness to Muslims. During the Hajj millions of Muslims from all over the world pay a short visit to Madinah (though it is not part of the Hajj to visit Madinah). They pray in the mosque and visit the areas which are associated with memories of the Prophet Muhammad and his companions.

Each time the name of the Prophet Muhammad is mentioned, Muslims pray "May the blessings and peace of Allah be upon him"

The Dome of the Rock

This golden domed building stands in the courtyard of
Al Aqsa Mosque in Jerusalem, surrounding the rock from which the
Prophet Muhammad ascended to Heaven on his Night Journey. The
outside walls are covered in turquoise patterned tiles. Round the top of
them are written all 83 verses of Surah Yasin, a chapter in the Quran.
You can walk round the mosque and read the whole chapter.

At the courtyard's front is the Al Aqsa Mosque itself. It is plainer. The
walls inside are pure white giving it a special peace and beauty.

How To Be Successful

The Quran keeps inviting us to do good so that we can be successful in this life and the next, and be safe from evil. It also has prayers for us to say, to help us become better people.

Here are some things believers should be doing:

1. Thanking Allah often.
2. Never missing prayers, and meaning them when we say them.
3. Giving to the poor, and helping anybody who needs help.
4. Being trustworthy and keeping our promises
5. Avoiding anger or complaining.
6. Always being humble, kind and courteous.
7. Forgiving people.
8. Never hating people or being jealous.
9. Living moderately, avoiding greed and luxury.
10. Being patient, and never calling people by bad nicknames.

Celebrating the Month Called Ramadan

During Ramadan Muslim adults fast during daylight hours, if they are well enough. Often younger Muslims want to fast too. Very young ones may be allowed to fast for a morning, to see what it is like.

Those fasting must have a meal (called *suhoor*) before dawn. Then during daylight we fast. We should break our fast immediately after sunset, even if we have only a sip of water and a couple of dates. Straight after the sunset prayer (*maghrib*) we enjoy a good meal. Breaking the fast is called *iftar.*

The main purpose of fasting is self-discipline, to help us behave well throughout the year and be grateful to Allah for the blessings He has showered upon us.

Fasting and *iftar* remind us of the people who don't have enough to eat. This encourages us to give money or food to the poor. The value of food becomes so alive at *Iftar*. Words praising Allah come rushing to our lips. At *iftar* the Prophet Muhammad would pray: " Praise be to Allah who helped me to keep my fast, who nourished me so that I could break my fast. Praise be to Allah; the thirst is quenched and the veins are moist. And by God's will our return is certain."

The Prophet Muhammad and the Old Lady

There was an old woman in Makkah who hated the Prophet Muhammad. Every morning when he passed by her house, she would empty a basket of rubbish on his head from the upper storey of her house. He never grumbled or said anything to her.

One day she was ill and in bed when he passed that way. Surprised that no rubbish had been emptied on his head, he thought, "She must be ill," and went upstairs to enquire how she was. The woman was very frightened. She thought he had come to quarrel with her.

When he said he had come to enquire after her health, she began to cry. "What a good man you are," she sobbed. "I ill-treat you and you enquire after my health. Teach me your religion. Teach me your way of life."

The Story of Two Gardens

Once there were two men. One of the men was rich and the other was poor. The rich man had two beautiful well-watered gardens with grape vines and date palms and he even had cornfields between the two gardens. He had lots of fruit in the gardens and grain in the fields. He thought all this was the result of his own efforts rather than a blessing from Allah.

One day he was showing the poor man round his gardens. Showing off, he said, "I am richer than you and I have far more people following me around. They think I'm great." Looking around his garden he said, "I don't think this will ever perish! - And I don't think there will ever be a Judgement Day, either." When the poor man heard him say this, he said, "Don't you believe in Him Who created you from dust, from something tiny, and then made you into a man? As for me, Allah is my Lord, and I will worship no one but Him. When you went into your garden all puffed up with pride, why didn't you say, 'It is as Allah wills: there is no power except with Allah'? - I'm saying this even if you do look down on me and my family because I'm poor." The very next day disaster struck. The gardens were laid waste. All the harvest was destroyed. The grapevines had collapsed on their trellises. The rich man wasn't rich any more. Wringing his hands in misery and shame, he cried, "If only I had worshipped no other gods beside my Lord!"

This story warns us never to think too much of ourselves, but to understand in all humility, "Whatever Allah has ordained must surely come to pass: there is no power except that of Allah."
(See the Holy Quran 18:32-46)

21

A Trip Called "Hajj"

Hajj takes place once a year. It is the pilgrimage made to Makkah in Saudi Arabia. Each year over two million Muslims from around the globe gather in Makkah for Hajj. The men wear two unstitched cloths called *ihram*. The women wear their normal clothes. They all walk around the Kabah seven times. Over and over again they say: "Here I am O Allah, here I am." The pilgrims also hurry seven times between two small hills near the Kabah. This reminds them of Prophet Abraham's wife running between these hills to find water to save her baby's life. The rites of Hajj take about a week, and the pilgrims stay in tents for part of it. One act of Hajj is to throw small stones at the pillars that represent Satan. This shows how believers should avoid temptation. One of the main acts of Hajj is to visit the hill of Arafat and stand there to say prayers. Here the Prophet Muhammad gave his historic sermon in which he said: "No black man is better than a white man, and no white man is better than a black man, except in how God-conscious he is!"

The Prophet's Message of Peace

A great part of the Prophet's mission was to bring peace to the world. One way of doing so was to remind people that all men and women, although living in very different regions of the world, and seemingly different from one another in colour, culture and language, etc., were in fact each other's blood brothers and sisters. The Prophet would preach to his followers: "You are all Adam's offspring and Adam was made of clay." And in his prayers to Allah, he would say, "O Lord, all your servants are brethren (brothers and sisters)." The Prophet himself set an example of peaceful living with his great gentleness, kindness, humility, and excellent common sense, and his great love for all people and for the animals too. He never made others feel small, unwanted or embarrassed. He urged his followers to do likewise.

This is expressed in one of the Prophet's sayings:

"Nine things the Lord has commanded me:
Fear of God in private and in public;
Justness, whether in anger or in calmness;
Moderation in both poverty and affluence;
That I should join hands with those who break away from me;
And give to those who deprive me;
And forgive those who wrong me;
And that my silence should be meditation;
And my words remembrance of God;
and my vision keen observation."

Sayings of the Prophet Muhammad ﷺ

- Paradise lies at the feet of mothers.

- Verily, Allah Almighty and His angels and those who inhabit the heavens, even the ants in their holes and the fishes in their waters, bless the good teachers of humankind.

- The best person among you is the one who treats his family members well.

- You should visit the sick, feed the hungry and set prisoners free.

- Pay the labourer his dues even before his sweat dries up.

- You are here to make things easy, not to make things difficult.

- You should refrain from making a promise and then going back on it.

- Every good act is charity.

- Modesty and chastity are parts of faith.

- Don't kill your hearts with excess of eating and drinking.

- The best of alms is that which the right hand gives and the left hand knows not of.

- All actions are judged by the motives prompting them.

- O Allah, I seek your protection from misery and grief; from weakness and laziness, and from the burden of loans and from things that might make others overcome me.

- O Allah, only You can change hearts. We beseech You to do so, so that we may submit to You.